Mrs Pat

by
Anton Burge

SERVING THEATRE

SF

SINCE 1830

WWW.SAMUELFRENCH.CO.UK
WWW.SAMUELFRENCH.COM

FOR AMATEUR PRODUCTION ENQUIRIES

UNITED KINGDOM AND WORLD EXCLUDING NORTH AMERICA
plays@SamuelFrench-London.co.uk
020 7255 4302/01

UNITED STATES AND CANADA
info@SamuelFrench.com
1-866-598-8449

Each title is subject to availability from Samuel French,
depending upon country of performance.

This text went to press during the rehearsal period and may differ slightly from what is presented on stage.

Author's Note

If a writer thinks of his plays as his children, then for me *Mrs. Pat* was the child who didn't want to leave home. First written over ten years ago, she went through various drafts, only to languish in the drawer marked unproduced. The piece was the first I ever wrote, and although other plays followed with larger casts, or more ambitious concepts, the idea of placing this – now somewhat forgotten – legend of the theatre in a monologue that focuses on a solitary night in her life, yet encompassing the whole of it, always caused me to hope that she might one day take her place centre stage.

I am delighted that Beatrice Stella Patrick Campbell, *Mrs. Pat*, has finally done so. Once considered the greatest actress of her time, she is now more remembered for her off stage wit, uneven temperament and devotion to her dogs. Yet there was so much more to a life that saw her create the first Paula Tanqueray and Eliza Doolittle, be a muse for George Bernard Shaw, appear in Shakespeare and Hollywood movies, and become one of the first actress-managers in the theatre. She worked alongside some of the greatest names in the business: Bernhardt, Forbes-Robertson and Beerbohm Tree, to name a few; she was a famed beauty, a champion of Ibsen, and somehow managed to combine a career that encompassed the progressive theatre with commercial West End triumphs. Her finances, though, were like her personality - unmanageable - and her glamorous public persona and sometimes malicious intellect (she was far too clever for the stuffed shirts she often found herself employed by or acting opposite), disguised the fact that she was hugely generous, supported husbands, family and friends, and paid her company well for their services. Such charity, changing fashions in the theatre, and running into trouble trying to smuggle her beloved dogs through customs took their toll on her career, and the end of her life was not the one such a trail blazer deserved.

My interest and admiration for the subject of this work is matched by Penelope Keith and Alan Strachan, without whom this project really would still be languishing in that drawer marked unproduced. And to them I offer my sincere thanks.

Anton Burge

October 2015

'*Mrs Pat*' was first produced by Chichester Festival Theatre at the Minerva Theatre, Chichester, on the 15th October 2015. The cast was as follows:

MRS. PATRICK CAMPBELL (STELLA) . . . . Penelope Keith

Director. . . . . Alan Strachan
Designer . . . . Simon Higlett
Lighting Designer. . . . . Jason Taylor
Sound Designer . . . . Gregory Clarke
Video Designer. . . . . Simon Wainwright
Puppetry Consultant . . . . Toby Olié
Costume Supervisor . . . . Karen Large
Wig Supervisor. . . . . Matt George
Production Manager . . . . Sam Paterson
Company Stage Manager. . . . . Robin Longley
Deputy Stage Manager. . . . . Christopher Lambert
Assistant Stage Manager . . . . Harriet Saffin

ANTON BURGE

Actor and writer Anton Burge has written eight plays for women, all focusing on the lives of celebrated women of the 19th and 20th centuries, including *Whatever Happened to the Cotton Dress Girl?*, *G & I* (both New End Theatre, Hampstead), *Bette & Joan*, starring Greta Scacchi and Anita Dobson (West End and UK tour) and *Storm in a Flower Vase* (West End), both for Ann Pinnington Productions. Future productions include *Lady Mosley's Suite* (read at the Trafalgar Studios with Patricia Hodge and Emilia Fox) and *Curtsey: The Gesture of an Inferior to a Superior* (read at The Soho Screening Room with Sophie Ward and Sylvestra le Touzel).

He is also the author of a forthcoming book, *Portraying Elizabeth*, a study of actresses' interpretations of Elizabeth I from Sarah Bernhardt to the present day, including interviews with Eileen Atkins, Glenda Jackson, Greta Scacchi, Anna Massey, Harriet Walter and Miranda Richardson.

He is working on a biography of Bette Davis, *A Life lived in Melodrama*, and his first contemporary play, *Year of the Virgin*.

A new production of *Bette & Joan* opens on Broadway next year, as well as productions opening in Spain and Germany.

Bette & Joan, *Storm in a Flower Vase* and *Mrs. Pat* are all published by Samuel French.

THANKS

The author would like to thank: Chichester Festival Theatre, Alan Strachan, Penelope Keith, Stephen Wicks, Emily Hayward, Deborah Smith, Sarah Wolf, Katie Langridge, Simon Higlett, Emma Anacootee-Parmar & Alix Harvey-Thompson.

The play is dedicated to the memory of Miss Mapp

For Penelope and Alan

CHARACTER

Mrs. Patrick Campbell (Stella): Legendary actress, imposing, temperamental, verbose. Once described as a relic of a bygone era, 75.

****

The play is set over the course of one night on a platform at Toulouse Station, France in 1940.

****

The music played throughout is:

Ravel's String Quartet – Section: Assez vif'. Très rythmé

ACT ONE

Winter 1940. Music. Sounds of trains, guards, whistles etc. Lights up very slowly: Toulouse Station in the evening. An announcement is made that the train from Toulouse to Pau will be delayed in arriving and to await further announcements. On a dim stage a bench is gradually lit; in the distance: porters' trolleys and luggage, and a waiting room just visible. The vast iron framework of the station rises up into the night. Situated next to the bench are a large, standing, travelling trunk, Three hat boxes – one of which is black and vast – a typewriter, smaller trunk and a small suitcase. Other pieces of luggage are nearby. Out of the noise the voice of **MRS. PATRICK CAMPBELL** **(STELLA)** *can be distinguished, calling for a porter.*

STELLA *(off)* Porter! ...Porter! ...Porter! *(etc... Silence for a moment.)*

STELLA *appears through the steam, a figure of decayed magnificence, in pursuit of the elusive porter. She wears a dark cloak with fur collar, upon which is pinned a bunch of wilting violets), a hat, and she carries an aging, monstrous looking Pekinese dog – Moonbeam – under one arm; her hands are encased in tattered gloves. She uses a cane (more for effect than necessity).*

Dear, dear... really! Porters today! Never to be had when one needs one; they are all prompt exits and no entrances! *(she enjoys her joke)* Naughty! I don't know why they shun me. Embarrassment? Recognition? Not wishing to be bathed in reflected glory? Yet, I am their friend, famed for the fact that I have always preferred porters to sentiment at railway stations! I could certainly use one now. *(spotting the porter again in the smoke)* Ah, there's the devil! *(she whips towards him, still clutching the overweight Moonbeam)* Porter! Don't elude me! Monsieur, then? *Monsieur!* *(she is snubbed)* Impudence – ignored! Even when addressed in their mother tongue! My fading charms play to an unresponsive audience, it would seem. *(she gravitates to the bench)* Such fickle people. The French. Of course we English have never taken to them.

1

(she removes her hat and places Moonbeam upon it, on the bench. Looking in the direction of the waiting room) Oh, oh, I see, I do have an audience. Of one! Like a wet matinee in Malvern. A lonely spinster, no doubt. Well, look, Madam, as much as you like: he is rather partial to crushed velvet – it makes for a better nap. I do hope she won't be travelling on the same train – I'm afraid any wish for companionship would only lead to disappointment. There, she has turned away. Au revoir! Such a gossipy nation. *(beat)* Damn this delay! I pray, though, it won't be cancelled. So few allowed to travel... but... well, we must hope! However, it is moments such as these that make one wonder if one can really stand up to this life.

She leans wearily against the trunk, as if it were a sort of lectern, and pats it gently.

(in profile:) I should be accustomed to it, I know: many are the hours I have endured such as these. But, this is different is it not? This isn't a linger at Crewe station – the waiting room there, full of the theatrical living dead, all passing the time before their connections! No, this is something much worse. This is... flight! This is escape! But I must calm myself. If only I had some oil of lavender... or a dash of something to steady my nerves. The step, the gesture, the word.

My lecture, yes... Yes! I will think of that. When I tour my lecture: *(she pushes the wheeled trunk centre and resumes her pose)* 'Mrs. Patrick Campbell on the Art of Acting and Beautiful Speech'. I am forever in such a predicament – waiting – and that is how I must see tonight, as merely one of life's predicaments, to be dealt with, overcome and laughed at. Like that stumble from the taxi cab, the leading man with sour breath or the fag, fag, fag of age!

When I tour my lecture, I travel not only over England, but also the United States of America, and many is the hour I have waited – with my poor Moonbeam – at the mercy of the organization of the transportation that goes by the appellation of the railways!

A beat. She looks about her; as she speaks the lighting changes to something more intimate and theatrical, as if she were addressing an audience.

I like to stand at my lectern, thus, in silhouette, keeping the head up, fashioning a better profile. I wear a white robe, pearls and have my hair up very high, and I always begin with Lady Macbeth "I have given suck!"

Though I wouldn't be doing any of it if I didn't have arrears to pay! Always borrowing from Peter to pay off Paul. No! I simply wouldn't.

I'm not sure the audience would either. They come for a glimpse of tattered splendour, I'll be bound, a taste of a bygone world. My beautiful self of recent memory, encased in what one now observes. The voice once compared to an instrument, now a basso profundo! And my gestures hailed for their grace and passion are ...imitated, even ridiculed.

But seesaw! Every one of us has to do it, even the sainted Ellen Terry, even dear Dame Ellen had to pack up her box of *maquillage* and go in search of monetary remuneration. The only one who didn't was that devil Alexander: he was shrewd, he was cunning. He was a fox! I wager George Alexander never saw Crewe station on a wet Sunday evening!

So, I push myself to the front of the stage, in the hope – for a moment at least – that the illusion will still pass muster...

During the course of my talk I speak of others who have brushed the hem of my career: some more classical than I, perhaps, others more... what is that American term? Oh, my memory... Legitimate! But none move or thrill an audience as I. When I want to. *(a beat)* Oh, yes, I am governed by demons, and sometimes they allow me to let the genie out the lamp, and sometimes... they don't.

Of this band of my theatrical brothers and sisters – for we mustn't forget the female of the species during my talks; experiencing greater obstacles to attain our moment in the sun – of the band I will not mention, Alexander. I refuse to, though he was a part of my life, I admit, regrettably... His arrogance still stings. I can tolerate much, but never arrogance!

Speaking of arrogance: I do mention Mr. George Bernard Shaw, the work, but not the ego, which I am sure would irritate dear Joey – I christened him Joey because he is such a pantomime clown! Though he can never see it. *(to herself)* And a devil not to let me have those letters. My letters! A devil not to let me publish our correspondence, so the world must, must read how he loved me, and cast me aside. Some may suggest he was in awe of my celebrity, granted. Some might say I only want to publish for the money – open to discussion. But should it not be read how love and adoration shift and alter as one celebrity rises, and the other falls. Those letters should be published as a warning to others!

(returning to her former style) I then favour my audience with some passable cockney – Shaw's Eliza Doolittle – after this I bash away at Lady Macbeth's sleepwalking scene, snippets of Juliet – not the tricky ones – and Ophelia. Then I give in to my listeners and complete my lecture with Paula Tanqueray. The mere mention of her name brings an ovation of appreciation. I know *The Second Mrs. Tanqueray* by Arthur Wing Pinero to be the greatest play of the last century. And so does my audience. This is more than a mere 'woman with a past' story. What a past! What a woman! Even Alexander, who produced, directed and – regrettably – cast himself as my husband in the original production, even he knew the part called for delicate handling from more than a mere actress of the day. They were all considered, trotted out like ponies, and cast aside as unsuitable, the search for Paula Tanqueray made the hunt for Scarlett O'Hara seem a mere glance about for a new chorus girl!

The success of the play changed my life forever. I was the toast of London! And like Miss Vivien Leigh now, a star. And much as he hated it Alexander was stuck with me… I was told later he kept a calendar and crossed the performances off until he was free of me! *(she laughs)*

Society picked me up! That genius Mr. Pinero introduced me to Mr. Beerbohm Tree, Mr. Tree introduced me to Burne-Jones, he to the Duchess of Rutland, she to the Hon. Mrs. Percy Wyndham; through her I met Mr. Aubrey Beardsley and he, well, he introduced me to Oscar Wilde. And on it went. Beardsley said Wilde was 'dying' to meet me, and why not, I ask you? The rest of London was. What do I care what these boys do as long as they don't do it in the streets and frighten the horses! I think Oscar was rather disappointed that my name was actually *Mrs.* Patrick Campbell: when I informed him

I truly did have a husband, he merely replied "How suburban!"
And I loved him ever after.

It seems a lifetime ago. And in fact is. Yet, I play her still. 'The
Second Mrs. Tanqueray' is still in my repertoire... though the
lines muddle me of late.

The sad reality of still playing Paula is that I have to say, about
another character in the play, "She's six and forty, and I wish
nothing worse to happen to any woman". But indeed there
are worse things that can happen to a woman: playing that
line night after night when you yourself are four and sixty! *(she
observes a porter pass. The lights revert to the station lighting as before)*
Yoo-hoo! Porter! Porter! *(she is too late)* Wretched man, what a
wretched, miserable, ugly, little man. Well, I care not – when
the train comes, they will have to wait a moment longer for
the rest of my luggage. *(she gestures with her stick, pointing it from
one spot of the platform to another)* If the train ever comes... many
are cancelled. Some materialize in disguise, appearing to go to
one destination, but actually on the way to another. No one it
seems can be trusted..., not even a train, any more. *(a beat)* It's
so shamefully cold... *(she moves about the platform to keep warm)*

I'm sure my lecture audiences think me very old hat – banging
on about sloppy diction and the lowering of standards. The
talkies are the worst – bring back silent pictures, I say! Most
actors are perfectly acceptable in silents. Except the ugly ones.
And poor speech is not just prevalent in the acting profession –
why, I was in church recently and the vicar tried to impress his
congregation with: *(imitates the vicar's nasal twang)* "Come unto
me, all ye who labour and are heavy laden, and I will give you
rest!" It was such a pity, as he was actually a rather beautiful
specimen. I told him afterwards – as I pushed the plate back –
"I would have left something, Father, but for the fact that you
opened your mouth!"

Joey, ahem *Mr.* Shaw, says I make up for everyone else by *over
articulating* myself! Still, it keeps us out there, don't you know.
What they call in the public eye. *(petting the dog as he sleeps)*
Doesn't it, Moonbeam, my beautiful baby, and it pays for any
little treat you might require. Besides, what does Joey know
about it? One can barely hear him as he mumbles into that
disgusting beard of his! No, if one has great things to say, then
better that they be audible. Even when dealing with members of

what is now termed 'The Press', I can't advise strongly enough: be clear, or one runs the risk of being misquoted! *(she edges the suitcase and a couple of her hatboxes about the platform as if they were members of her audience. Her attention moves from one to the next and back again. Sounds of chatter, popping flashbulbs; occasionally she poses for her picture)* I like to scatter these reporters about me – not too close – and remind them great artistry is acquired through instinct rather than profession. Anyone can work at it. Few of us are born.

Grandly she sits on the bench next to Moonbeam; the lights change, moving from box to box etc. as STELLA*'s attention moves with each question.*

I suppose it is only natural that people should be fascinated, but, sometimes such curious questions are darted at me: from the American Motion Picture Star: Have I met Ruth Chatterton? "Well, yes", I reply, "as a matter of fact I have", though I didn't know her from Adam. "She is a famous moving picture star", I was told. Not quite top drawer, in my opinion. "What are my favourite flowers and scent?" from *The Daily Telegraph* is much more to my liking. "Violets," I answer. "And scent? The bouquet of sweet Moonbeam's paw". And my favourite question: "Who is your preferred leading man?" I reply, as I always do: "Why, Madame Sara Bernhardt, of course!" I had a real stinger recently, not from the Press at all, but from a young schoolgirl, loitering at the stage door, with her mother. *(she addresses the upright suitcase)* "Where do you find the inspiration to play so many wicked women?" I mean, really! *(her gaze shifts again)* And from Le Figaro, of course, those scandalmongers, "How old are you?" *(she bristles)* I find when it comes to age a perfectly good sticking point is forty! Even if that does make my children illegitimate!

(she rises and the lights revert to the general light of the platform) Of course, what they always ask is: how did it all begin? *(gestures with her cane)* How did I get from there to here? And how did I?

Born Beatrice Rose Stella Tanner, in Kensington, on February the 9th – I don't tell them 1865 – making me an Aquarius: a diplomat, and a talker. I was the baby of a family of six: wearing other people's costumes is second nature to me. My father was English, my mother a romantic Italian. From her I inherited a love of beauty. And from him, the ability to lose fortunes! He spoke not a word of Italian, she not an utterance of English. I can recommend no finer formula for marriage! I grew up neither sweet nor amiable, am impatient with fools and yet – and this is the truest fact about me – I am made up of three parts fool.

When I decided that the stage was my calling, if one intended to be a respectable actress, as I most certainly did, one used one's married name, as did Mrs. Theodore Wright, Mrs. Beerbohm Tree, Mrs. Kendle, Mrs. *Kemble* and so I... I became Mrs. Patrick Campbell. Now, however, it is merely 'Mrs. Pat'– 'Mrs. Pat'. A term of massive affection, I know. I always insist on *'Mrs. Patrick Campbell'* whenever I am billed, though. Why, only recently, while in Hollywood making a talkie – don't you know, such a vulgar experience – Mr. Irving Thalberg, the head of the studio Metro Goldwyn Mayer, enquired if I would be billed as Stella Campbell! "Stella Campbell!" I replied. "If May Whitty can smack Dame before her name" – a Dame for her charity appearances, I believe, not for art – "I'm sure I can be a simple 'Mrs.'!"

I was making a picture with Mr. Thalberg's wife, Norma... something or other... Shearer, I think? It's not of importance, though I was told she was the leading lady at the studio. "Are you sure?" I replied. "Oh, yes," I was informed. "She works tremendously hard." I could only imagine. *(she collects up Moonbeam)* Of course, the real leading player was Moonbeam. You were marvellous in it, my angel. I make sure he's in all my pictures, whatever the story.

As she speaks the lighting creates the effect of a bright follow spot, a projector runs.

But, oh, the lights, the early hours, making one look older than God, and the obtuse people! *(fade in party music)* Mr. Thalberg asked me, after the screening party – an inglorious affair – what I thought of his wife. "Well, Mr. Thalberg," I said "She's quite, quite charming, such a dainty creature." "Oh, yes, she is," replied he. "Such tiny hands," said I. "Oh, yes, she has," he agreed, warming to me at last – I could taste another contract coming my way. "And such a tiny waist," I continued. "Yes, hasn't she?" He purred, to which I added: "And such tiny, tiny,

tiny eyes!" I haven't worked with them since! Well, how was I to
know she had a stye? Not that it matters – Hollywood bores me.
I've made other pictures there, but they don't want my style of
'Art', they just want Jean Harlow, and we all know what that
name can be confused with!

The follow spot and music dim.

I believe, and I tell my lecture audience this always, "beautiful
speech is a habit of mind, an art and a personal matter" And
most of the people connected with talkies have no art! Why,
a cameraman, on the last picture I made there, called me
"Babe!" Babe! The ignominy of it. He then presumed to ask
of Moonbeam "What's the little feller's name?" "Titty Bottles!"
I replied, which seemed to shut him up! *(as she speaks she
replaces Moonbeam on her hat momentarily, then picks up the small
suitcase, puts it on the bench, props it open and places him inside
it, wrapping him in a coverlet)* This beastly cold. Must we wait
here all night? Don't the French understand I have treasure
to transport? Such an inconsiderate nation... rather like the
Americans. *(she sits on the bench)*

"A screen test, Mrs. Campbell, you'll have to undergo a screen
test, if you want to go to Hollywood," my agent had informed
me. *(she turns on the bench and her face picks up the light; again, the
projector runs)* With my chin of sixteen dewlaps, I was declared a
ruin! As I left the sound stage I heard the cameraman mutter,
"And you say she was known as a beauty? She looks like a burst
paper bag!" *(pause. She stares into the light)* It is hard to reconcile
the eye's memory to the reality of what is now staring back at it.
I never regret the loss of my looks, I just regret the expectation
of them: as the curtain rises, yet another audience's memories
are shattered! *(the lights change. She rises angrily)* Screen tests
indeed! I, who have played opposite Bernhardt, made Ibsen's
name and been loved by that scoundrel Mr. Bernard Shaw! I,
who have been muse to Shakespeare, Ibsen, Pinero, Sardou!
And Hollywood insists I make a screen test!

Perhaps I should submit to the challenge of a cosmetic surgeon,
like that fright Mary Pickford: she can't snap her mouth open,
but gee, does she look swell in them close ups!

*She opens the trunk. It is crammed with clothes, letters, books and other
memorabilia all spilling over. She pulls a hand mirror from a drawer.*

Though I'm sure there would be many willing to pay for a surgeon to keep my mouth firmly shut! *(as she looks at her reflection)* Ah, yes, it is unfortunately as I remembered. Yet I was beautiful. I was known as a beauty, if not for my charm. And the beautiful always get help, however foolish they might be. *(she replaces the glass)* Some of the vestiges remain. *(beat)* Besides, what do I care?

(chuckles as she looks at the contents of trunks) Oh, look at it all! Will you look at it, Moonbeam. The rumble-tumble of my life. My trouble is I don't have anyone to pack for me any more – such a nuisance! The budget won't allow it. Now, each time I travel I have to buy another trunk for all the things I can no longer stuff into the last! Of course this is nothing to when I toured America, when I was known as an 'event' as well as a beauty!

So hard for us to travel on our own... and with this wretched war... Selfish of the Germans, interfering with our lovely plans. *(she rises, rubbing her hands together)* Still, if we can get to Pau I shall feel safer. And the Parisians are such gossips, always winkling for scandal. I shall be glad to see the back of them. It is not cowardice that makes us flee – I have never been a coward – it just makes sense, for everyone in fact, to leave. And the owner of the pension was so adamant that we had to go, that all his patrons must leave as soon as they could get their belongings together. Tears in his eyes, at the loss of Moonbeam and myself. Fear in his heart. *(beat)* I don't understand why the Jews don't take flight. They are welcome in Hollywood. Unfortunately we can't get home – they won't let us. Not the Germans, this beastly quarantine law! So here we are: France's rendering of Crewe Station. Toulouse at night. These are sinister times, Moonbeam. Even a fool like myself can perceive that, sinister times... *(she looks about her. Strokes Moonbeam)* You want the chicken, don't you? From the maitre d' at the Pension. Generous in his praise of you, and such worship of me! But I can't think where it could have gone!

She searches her person and some of the untidy trunk drawers. She finds a folded napkin containing some past-their-best grapes.

Not the chicken, but a remnant of the hot house, a treasure of the vine, that he knows I adore. Packed secretly... intimately! Without my knowledge. Wayward youth. *(looking at the decaying fruit)* I love fruit – especially when it's expensive. *(she sighs)* If only they were prop grapes, at least they would look appetizing. *(she places the napkin in a drawer. In doing so she comes across a large sheet of paper)* Well, well, what have we here? Who would have thought! I presumed this was lost years ago! *(opening the paper)* Touring with Madame Sara Bernhardt. The 9th to the 30th of September, 1905. Well, well... how easy it is to let one's life unravel. I was Melisande to her Pelleas. *(holding it to her breast)* She was a marvel, such energy, passion, dedication! My dear Sara, after all these years. Where are you now, now when I need your resourcefulness, your genius... your generosity? Sara would never have let herself travel third class and found herself stuck here. She was so far thinking: always seeing herself as a business as well as an artist. She didn't hold with this new wave drama sweeping across Europe from Scandinavia. No time for it, she said. Her audiences wanted majesty, tragedy, drama! And she gave them it in spades. *(beat)* 'The Divine Sara.' The seventh wonder of the world! I should have been jealous of her! But I could only watch in awe and applaud. I remember the last time I saw her: she was in her dressing room, making up before a performance. A performance! – She was an old woman and could barely walk after the leg amputation – I asked her why she bothered to apply make-up to her fingers? *(STELLA bends as if speaking to someone making-up in a mirror)* "No one will notice!" I said. "Have another cake" – How she loved England's buns! – Then she replied very seriously, the voice of genius: "I shall notice, and that is all that matters." *(beat)* Later we dined together. She was ailing terribly, had to be carried upstairs, by some young lover, and as they turned the corner, that frail, yet undefeatable body, raised an arm, and kissed the tips of her fingers to me...and I knew, I knew it was the last time... *(beat)* Such memories! Such exquisite memories. And so rare, two leading ladies! The audiences adored us.

Her brilliance was the ability to reinvent herself: when there weren't enough female roles to satisfy her, she would play male leads instead! Inspirational. None of us came close. *(she reads from the paper, as the lights intensify. Distant sounds of trains)* The itinerary for the British Tour of 'Pelleas & Melisande': Leave London, Euston; matinee & evening in Birmingham; the next day matinee in Wolverhampton, evening performance in Leamington; then Nottingham, Sheffield, Manchester,

Liverpool. Sunday, sail for Dublin. Tuesday, sail for Fleetwood. Then: Blackpool, Bradford and Hull! After which the Divine Sara sailed for Paris, where, no doubt, she performed *Hamlet* that evening! *(lays down the paper. Opens another drawer, searching for the nibble for Moonbeam)* Now, where is it? How can it be lost amongst such a supreme degree of organization? In a white napkin, I believe he put it in a crisp, white napkin for you. I hoped there would be enough for the both of us...

Music. The lights dim as STELLA *rummages for the chicken. Train announcements and sounds of trains arriving and leaving the station become louder. She looks up, then returns to what she is doing, disappointed by the delay. Smoke, steam etc. She pushes the trunk open further and not finding the chicken begins to sort through some letters poking from one of the internal drawers; she removes the small drawer and places it on her lap.*

Oh Moonbeam, at least when we get to Pau things will be quieter, and safer. One hears such stories... such horror! Can it be true? Can it? Paris lacks the dignity it once had, the beauty, the *éclat*. All this trouble has seen to that, the poor people, and I, poor coward, am too old to stay and fight alongside them. The fight of life is more pressing: the poverty, the discomfort, and nobody to offer you and I an arm to cross the road, not even that – and the traffic is so truly terrifying. *(she wipes her eyes)* At least in Pau there may be someone who appreciates us. We can't go home, not if those beasts at quarantine have breath in their bodies! No, we can't go home...

(brighter) And in Pau, at least we shall be near the border... and a room will be cheaper. Éclairs less expensive. That is always of the utmost necessity these days. Strange to think I used to run two households and make contributions to a third, and now I'm lucky if I can afford a second room for a maid. Not that I can afford the maid to pop in it... *(as she sorts letters)* But no moping, we won't have moping, will we? It's so bad for the forehead... Is it here? No? Just letters and my life.

(she notices the handwriting on one) Ah, Pat. Pat. The man whose name I bear. No, I can't read it, won't read it: a letter from a young man called Patrick Campbell, who put paid to any early dreams of the theatre. *(she reads)* Love took their place. Fool that I am, I have always had a fondness for love. I will never

forget Mother's heartbroken face. Daughters can be so very cruel.

We were such fools to marry on a mere £200 a year. People are very modern today about money, they say it does not matter: "Oh that!" They say, "What of it?" But money, money has always mattered, and it always will. I've spent my entire life borrowing from Peter to pay off Paul.

She gestures as if moving money from one cloak pocket to the other. She jumps up, knocking the letters to the platform floor.

Aha! Not the chicken, but coconut ice! Rather delicious if one remembers to remove the fluff! Moonbeam, it will give your wife sustenance to search once more for food for her master! *(she nibbles and sits again)* And a soupçon for you? *(preoccupied over the next section with her own thoughts, Moonbeam fails to get any)*

It is strange how thoughts return to those at the back of one's mind, yet the thoughts at the front remain in such disorder. Oh, poor Pat, poor boy, he really shouldn't have married me, but he did love me so.

He worked as an insurance clerk, in the City, while I stayed at home and watched the debts grow, and my fancies of a better life collapse. To top it all I became pregnant. I was told I was entering into a 'blooming' time for a woman. So common! I found neither it, or myself, blooming to any degree. I was sick of the poverty, sick of being the wrong side of the Thames, sick of having to borrow from the landlady. It sends a lump to my throat just remembering all those dreams of society I once had.

(she rises) I was Mr. Shaw's liberated Eliza, the other legendary role of my career:

(ladylike) "I should just like to take a taxi to the corner of Tottenham Court Road and get out there and tell it to wait for me, just to put the girls in their place. I wouldn't speak to them, you know. You don't call the like of them my friends now, I should hope. They've took it out of me often enough with their ridicule when they had the chance; and now I mean to get a bit of my own back."

(she laughs, then suddenly) And then, like an epiphany, a strength seemed to enter my soul and I knew that the responsibility of mine and my child's life was mine alone; I knew I must *never* be afraid again and that I must *work, work, work!* I could no longer rely on my dear despondent Pat. But isn't that true of all men? I became brave... it's only now that fear creeps back again...

Pause. STELLA *begins to pace up and down, blowing on her hands to keep warm. Music.*

One of the questions I am often asked after my talks is: Of the actresses of today, whom do I admire? And I always reply "Me!" And why not? I see nobody to follow me, or Ellen Terry or dearest Sara. Certainly not Norma... Norma? I forget. My memory... learning lines can become a... The one with the squint! That's it. No! The stye! Norma Whats-her-name! Well, certainly not her! Eleanora Duse, a so-called contemporary, but so uncivillised, certainly not her. I saw her as Hedda Gabler, not a patch on mine, and wished she'd shot herself at the first interval! Strange woman – she once asked to borrow the sets of a production I owned. I said of course, I lent them for nothing, requesting only a ticket for the performance as payment. When I reached the theatre I was handed a bill. For my ticket! On reaching my seat I was presented with a box of gardenias, a nice touch, thought I – to make up for the charge of the ticket, no doubt – and I modestly enquired whom the flowers were for? I was instructed to throw them on the stage when Madam Duse took her Second Act bow! I took them home in a taxi cab!

But notoriety doesn't make a great artist! It takes work, dedication, sacrifice. I soon found that out when my dear Pat – finding little success in the city – left to make his fortune in South Africa. He was gone for seven years! So I became an actress.

Once I had admitted my calling to my art, what was there to stop me? Beo *(pronounced 'Bayo')* my baby son, meaning 'Beloved One', was followed by baby Stella, and so I had to support them both myself, there was no chance of the elusive African gold finding its way back to us.

My days were spent in rehearsals, my evenings on stage and my nights making my costumes. Oh, the fag of it all. Dreary

hours, shabby lodgings, filthy food and always the milk train to
the next engagement. But despite what one critic called 'No
technique and the voice of a singing mouse', engagements
began to follow, and I steadily became known an artist of
repute, though even today actresses are never thought of as
quite the ticket, and often rightly so, look at Miss Tallulah
Bankhead! Currently enjoying huge success both sides of the
Atlantic. Skating on thin ice – and everyone wants to be there
when it breaks!

The lights brighten. **STELLA** *removes her gloves and tidies her hair,
smoothes down her cloak. In time, street sounds fade in and out.*

I had gained an introduction to the theatrical agent, a
Mr. Harrington Baily, the only one I had heard of. On locating
the office, however, I heard the pitiable mewing of a cat.
On glancing at the gutter, I found a mother cat washing her
drowned kittens! All of them dead! It was pitiable, pitiable. The
sight broke my heart – the lives of our four legged friends has
always been of a greater concern to me than those of our two –
many are the appointments I refuse for fear of neglecting my
darling baby, with his delicate health and weak eyes...

I digress. Upon entering the office, I opened my mouth
to speak and burst into a flood of tears. "I'm Mrs. Patrick
Campbell," I exclaimed, "from the Norwood Players... I've got
a letter of intro... I'm so sorry, just a little upset... You see
there is a... *Ah, Ah...* Oh, thank you, yes, I would like a cup of
tea." *(she steadies herself, sits on a suitcase and is wreathed in smiles)*
I finished my tea and composed myself and was informed that
Mr. Harrington Baily, such a pleasant man, was producing a
play called 'Bachelors', and needed a leading lady, who was
able to cry – I think I had heard that somewhere... *(beat)* There
were those who said that the incident of the mother cat in the
gutter never happened, but I chose to ignore such tittle-tattle.
People are so green eyed.

My London debut caused something of a sensation, and not
for all the reasons one would wish. My dresser, a slattern of
dubious repute, was having difficulty with the ties of my skirt, a
dark raggedy creation with fastenings at the back. To aggravate
my mounting hysteria she kept addressing me as "Dear", which
simply made matters worse! When my call came, I found myself

about to face my first London audience petrified, vulnerable and wearing a costume that could fall down at any moment!

She rises. The lights dim, the faint sound of an audience, which grows and reacts to the incident on stage and then becomes applause.

I am in the wings, the terror mounting, my heart pounding. My moment comes. I enter – and, of course, during my most important speech, my skirt falls down. There I stood in my white drawers with blue ribbons, the audience tittering, the gallery calling, but I knew, I knew I must carry on. Gathering my skirt about me, I played with such vigour, such strength, that I earned from that audience my first ovation, and their respect for life. *(she makes her curtsey)* I had never known such applause... never felt such warmth... such... love. *(beat)* And those scandal mongers, who cast aspersions about cats in gutters, and suggest that I dropped my skirt by intent, may I remind them it takes more than effect to sustain a career as long, or successful, as mine!

Train announcements. Music.

Disappointment again. And so we wait. Strangers brought together in limbo, on the set of a station, all artifice, as we wait to depart. *(she watches the occasional passerby, meets their gaze)* The people who recognize me now, wonder one of three things: how I got so portly, how I became so old, or what the hell am I doing here! Quite often I get calling cards from gentlemen I haven't seen in over forty years, gentlemen who say they will see the performance and take me to dine afterwards. More often than not they stay for the first curtain – where I take a bow before my public, often in the harshest of lights – and later I find myself dining alone! Gentleman of a certain age are in such great demand at about nine o'clock in the evening, it would seem!

Others stay though, and come round and see me afterwards. Why, young John Gielgud, only recently, such a pet, and talented too – he's beginning to make something of himself – attempted to interest me in a play about an ex-opera singer who spends her time making spaghetti and hiding her daughter who has had an illicit affair. I said to him "I suppose, John, dear, you want me to play the daughter?"

(she rises, the lights flicker, as in a Victorian melodrama) When you've
been a success from the beginning, as I was after playing Paula
Tanqueray, it's hard to consign oneself to portraying ex-opera
singers! Yet, though success opens many doors, it also locks
them behind you.

The Second Mrs. Tanqueray – the story of a new wife with
a scandalous past – was a part other actresses feared or
misunderstood. Suffragettes may have balanced life out for us,
but the Paulas of this world still exist, and, alas, continue to.
Whether that oaf George Alexander realized this, who knows?
What he did comprehend as my leading actor and manager,
was that he had a hit on his hands, and I was about to make
him a whole stash of money!

As the curtain fell on the first night, and the audience sat
shocked and silent, I had no idea of the legend I was creating.
But my success came from Paula's sorrow, I never forget that,
even now, all these years later, when I play her still, I never
forget Paula and her dilemmas are with us everywhere:

(recites) "You kill me with this life! What is my existence? A drive
to the village to give my orders to the trades people, a game of
bezique you and I. Then a yawn from me, another from you.
'Goodnight' 'Goodnight' Ah! And so we will go on here, year
in and year out, until the sap is run out of our lives..." *(she takes
a bow)*

Ah, poor Paula Tanq, but such is wedlock: the deep, deep
peace of the double bed after the hurly-burly of the chaise-
longue!

(she goes to close the drawer only to discover the chicken) Moonbeam!
The chicken! We may feast like kings! *(she munches and talks,
forgetting to share any with Moonbeam)* And how I heard they
feasted that night, the first night party of 'Tanqueray' – without
me! Even Alexander, even he was said to drink to my success,
and my absence! George Alexander: actor, manager, miser,
snob, bully, prude and pompous ass, now I must come to him.
(finishing the last piece of chicken) Oh, Moonbeam, not hungry
after all? Too much excitement, no doubt. *(the lights close in)*
And there was too much excitement during the rehearsals
for 'Tanqueray'. It was a wonder we ever made it to the stage!
Rehearsals would break down every two or three pages.

Dear Mr. Pinero, the author, would tell me "Here is where, in your anger, you sweep all the bric-a-brac and photographs from the piano". "Mr. Pinero, I do not feel I can make her throw everything from the piano in such a manner." Silence then greeted me. Mr. Pinero edges his way backwards through the stalls, and the safety of the foyer. Mr. Alexander then speaks: "Mrs. Campbell, it does not matter what you feel or do not feel. Please play the scene as Mr. Pinero intended". "Mr. Pinero, Mr. Pinero, can you hear me? I appeal to you. You do see, don't you? It just doesn't follow with my interpretation". Alexander then pipes up again. I turn my back and laugh at his baboon red face! "I thought you would be pleased," I say to him. "It will save you pounds and pounds on props each night! Now what do you say, Mr. Pinero?" Mr. Pinero, running for a cab, calls, "Do as you like my child!" Such a pet. And I do. I do do as I like. And Alexander lets me. For even he, even *he*, knew that I was right.

During the run I was presented with a card from Mr. Alexander's dresser. "Dear Mrs. Campbell, my compliments and will you please refrain from laughing at me on stage". I told his dresser to wait, and presented him with a card: "My compliments to Mr. Alexander and please tell him that I never laugh at him until I get home!" *(she roars with laughter)* And that was the last time we spoke to the other!

Alas, the result of all this, the strain of fame, and the fatigue of playing in an arduous long run, was a stretch at a nursing home. But I rallied – I always do; I have suffered many such stretches, many such nursing homes…

When I left the St. James' – Alexander sent me a note, after my last performance: "Mrs. Campbell, you are magnificent, yet unmanageable!" Stale news! I took an offer from the actor Johnston Forbes-Robertson and moved to his Lyceum Theatre to play Juliet, not the tricky speeches, to his Romeo. Such a noble profile and deep, manly voice. I blush to admit it, but… I fell in love. Deserted though I was, I should have resisted… Johnston took me seriously. I was his equal, on stage and off. If I was a new woman, he understood that and became a new man. I was part of him, and he me. Everything was golden: my health improved, my life and my work were entwined, and all was sunny in the garden.

Then Pat sent word he needed money to return home... The girl he had left had become the toast of London and mistress to one of its most acclaimed actors, and was somebody he no longer knew. Dusty, shabby, tired, he stood in the doorway of my new life, and all I wanted was for him to turn around again.

Oh, why must a woman always sacrifice and do the decent thing?

As for Forbes he told me his heart would always remain my footstool...

Only once did I hear that he spoke of me again: he passed my painting in the Royal Academy and whispered, "Ah, that little woman, that Juliet." *(she sits. The light closes in)*

After more time at a nursing home – love and theatre are cruel bedfellows – Pat decided to leave me again and fight in the Boer War.

(picking up Moonbeam and cradling him) Oh Moonbeam, darling boy, my little husband, it's all such an age ago... Joey says that the best thing that could happen would be for you to pass away so that I might resume my career in England or the United States. He says to put myself out there and play 'Eccentric Aunts' and 'Comedy Turns'. I mean, really! As if I care! And can I be bothered? *(props open a small case and places Moonbeam inside to sleep)* Joey should know better than to make me choose: he is such an odious old ponger, just like those wretched custom officials. I've written to the King about them, and the Prime Minister! Why must everyone want to separate me from the one thing that has never let me down? We're reduced to smuggling you through as part of my fur collar. But it's getting rather tricky: one gains a reputation at customs if one's breast barks!

Pause as further announcements etc. are made. **STELLA** *stands by the trunk, her palm upon it. Music.*

Unmanageable? I decided to manage myself! If a man can do it, why not a woman? Thus 'Mrs. Patrick Campbell's Company' opened at the Royalty Theatre and as the war blazed I packed them in.

Each night, during the intervals of the play, the audience would rush from their seats to read the latest war news pasted on the news boards outside. One night, as I was taking my bow, I spotted my uncle in the wings... And I knew... knew what had happened. *(beat)* Pat was a good man, a kind man and he truly loved me, and in spite of my behaviour. My brave, gentle Pat. *(pause. Rises)*

I closed the theatre for a week. I couldn't for any longer. I'm a hopeless book keeper, and lavish sets, and the best actors cost money. My answer to debt, remains the same to this day: go on tour in a lovely new play. If only more writers thought the same way. Why only the other day I ran into Emlyn Williams, poor boy, who proudly told me he had just finished a *'translation'* for that loathsome Edith Evans – who seems to be getting all the parts I should – and what did I think? A translation? I said to him: "Emlyn dear, I have a spiffing idea – why not write a new play, out of your very own head, for a poor, penniless harridan who really *can* act!"

Perhaps if I had been more frugal, like that miser Alexander, the company might have fared better? But money, I believe, belongs to those that need it most. Joey says that even if he were to send me £500 tomorrow to help my present predicament, it would only last me a week! If only he would give me the chance to prove him wrong. Therefore, when Queen Victoria died, and all the theatres were forced to close, there was only one thing for me to do. One thing! Bankrupt and widowed as I was, I followed the fashion of my peers, and sailed, sailed, sailed away... on a lovely tour, in a lovely new play, to America! *(she stares resolutely out, as the lights fade. Music)*

End of Act One

ACT TWO

Later that evening. Music. Lights up. STELLA *without her cloak (tossed aside) has added a vibrant, worn, winter shawl to her costume and stands in profile behind the bench. The station seems deserted. A copy of* Hedda Gabler *lies open on top of a number of scripts on the main trunk. Other items have been replaced. Moonbeam sleeps in his cushioned case.* STELLA *deep in concentration, one hand on her hip, a pistol in the other, raised hand. She is practicing imaginary shots, counting, slowly, quietly...*

STELLA One, two, three, four, five, six, seven. Fire! *(she pretends to fire, drops her arm then raises it again)* One, two, three, four, five, six, seven. Fire! *(she looks about her)* Well, what else is one to do on an empty platform? *Hedda Gabler*, Act One, Scene One. Completely unorthodox, I know, and not what Mr. Ibsen wrote at all, but, perhaps what Mr. Pinero would have, and certainly what Mrs. Campbell directed! To be a great artist one has to be original! *(she toys with the pistol)* And this might come in handy one day. Who knows, my dear? *(she puts the pistol away. Beat)* Further delays it seems. I'm beginning to wonder if we shall ever reach Pau. Or must I end my days here? For we can't go back, not to Paris, not with the Nazis on their way. Almost there! Horrible! With their Wagner and their nasty goosefleshing and their ideals – horrible! They won't take kindly to the likes of us, will they Moonbeam? *(she picks up Moonbeam and he snuffles into her breast)* No, no, we can't go back. *(a beat. She lets Moonbeam sit on her hat again)* And besides there don't seem to be any wretched trains! *(beat)* If only the Americans would help the British. There was talk of it when I was there... They may not all be civilized, certainly not in Hollywood, but they do know how to get things done!

(putting Hedda Gabler *away, waving it a little, remembering:)* America loved *Hedda Gabler*. I wasn't sure that they would. She is the thorny jewel in Ibsen's crown. And boredom is hard to play. Often one is bored to death on stage, at least I can be,

but one should never play it! So for Hedda, I took to moving the furniture about: mad bursts of energy damped down with physical exertion. The Americans went wild for it! And not just for Hedda, for Paula Tanqueray, and Agnes Ebbsmith – in fact all of my triumphs! But most importantly, America loved me! *(she sits)* So successful were those early tours that I broke records in New York and Chicago! Almost bankrupt, but not quite, I was now able to send money to those damn creditors at home – I owed nearly £12,000, don't you know – but, though I made a fortune, I still managed to return broke.

She sighs, rises and collecting her cloak, she tosses it about her shoulders. The lights change. We hear the pop of flashbulbs and the blur of a crowd of reporters and fans.

For my first appearance on American soil, I descended the gang plank wearing sables and an air of triumph! Then the journalists began. *(she addresses each)* "Mrs. Campbell, do you wear stays when you perform?" "What do you think of the Black Bottom?" "Mrs. Campbell, did you acquire your fortune from Campbell Soup?" By this time I had had enough! I told my secretary. "Tell them anything – except my age!"

(as she removes her cloak) And so it would continue. I toured America whenever I was hard up, spent prolifically, returned home, fell into debt and toured again! Back in England my magic was beginning to expire, as my waistline increased. I was out of plays, parts and inspiration! Darling Beo, my boy, now a man, was some help, when he announced he wanted to become a playwright. I told him, write your mother a divine hit play that will run a week in the provinces and get me back to the West End. Alas, the fate of the tour de force: she is always forced to tour!

(a pause) Perhaps there will be a producer in Pau? Willing to invest in a former enchantress with dropsy! The last producer I dealt with in England said it was always difficult employing a high salaried actress in a small theatre; I told him go find me a larger theatre then! I bet they never said that to Alexander! Or Forbes-Robertson. Not marrying him was a mistake, I see that now… What a chance-medley this life is! How very different for a man in my position. We have the vote now, thanks to the Sisterhood, but does it really bring us eye to eye with our

husbands, brothers, lovers, leading men? *(she turns and sits on the bench)*

I saved on actors' salaries by employing Beo – who said he now wished to be an actor, as playwriting was not for him – and such a loss I had to endure because of it. While in America, across the footlights, a young American – American no less – took a shine to my darling.

Helen. *Helen.* A name I have never liked – I have always been guided by such presentiments. She was of a decent pedigree, trade of course, but not enough pedigree to bring a feather to the family cap, and oh, so naïve! She once interrupted a rehearsal of *Electra* – I was working at home, so much cheaper than hiring rooms – to inform me that we had run out of lavatory paper! I would say to Beo – before their divorce, such a creditable innovation – I would say, "I can't think what is the matter with her? I allow her to live with us" – too generous I know – "yet, she runs about the place, screaming, positively screaming at the top of her voice! And sometimes Beo, my dear, I can even decipher my name in the racket!" I don't think she quite understood the fondness a mother can have for her son…

An announcement. **STELLA** *rises, listening attentively. It is not her train to Pau. She watches a small bustle of passengers. She returns to the bench, goes to Moonbeam, looks at him asleep, then arms folded she walks up and down, kicking her skirts. Music.*

I'm surprised anyone gets anywhere. Poor lighting, power restrictions and fear permeating the air… The war has put shot to anything running on time, little information, and then sometimes incorrect… In England I hear they don't even have the names of the stations displayed anymore… And in Austria the Nazis force the women to scrub the streets. The streets! Can it be true? Will the French allow this also? Not in Pau, Surely not! I couldn't do it. I wouldn't be able to bend. *(beat)* Though I doubt we shall be there for long… Or anywhere for that matter… What do you think Moonbeam?

(a pause) Beo's divorce cost me a fortune, though I have never spent money more willingly. The result was I was forced to play Vaudeville! I topped the bill in Chicago, our play performed between 'Acrobats Extraordinary' and a group of performing

seals. How the arc of one's career soon shifts to the downward slide. But what was I meant to do? People don't want Art any more: they would rather go to the 'flicks'. And I am that modern phenomenon: a working woman, who has debts to pay.

Short pause. She walks to the stage/platform edge.

If only there was a little comfort left in the world for us.

A maid! That would make up for a lot. Someone to cook for me. I get so hungry. *(retrieving the envelope of chicken in her skirt pocket. Offering it)* Moonbeam? *(Moonbeam carries on sleeping and* **STELLA** *proceeds to eat some)* I should like some macaroni, a salad, cheese, Devonshire cream, fruit and good brown bread… and, yes, I have to admit it, Joey for company. *(she moves back from the edge and sits on the arm of the bench)* I suppose he thinks me too old and ugly to be spoken to… He was not in love with me, I see that now. He loved my celebrity – such a common thing to emulate – and how it helped ignite his own. *(beat)* Oh, why hasn't he helped? I want to work, to work before the magic slips away.

And when I think of the parts he based on me: 'Apple Cart', 'Heartbreak House', not forgetting Cleopatra. Yet, was I allowed to play them? Never! "You will ruin them", he would say. Impertinence of it. Yet he was another who laid his heart at my feet to rest upon. No! To walk upon! He now feels exploited by me. Me! I who have influenced his work like no other. And he won't even let me publish our letters, he'd rather see me starve in the gutter and beg for food for my Moonbeam, for fear his words upset Mrs. Shaw! Well, what do I care? He shouldn't have written them, if that were the case, and they are my letters too. "Doesn't your conscience prick you?" I wrote him. But he failed to reply. I should sell his letters – they are all here! People tell me to! *(she rushes to the large black hat box)* I could earn myself a fortune! He'd be furious! *(claps her hands with glee)* Why shouldn't I sell? The correspondence of our lives, the love and abuse of many years. *(reading from a letter plucked randomly)* "Stella, Stella! I kiss your hands and praise Creation for you! O beautiful illustrious! O sweet of body and kissable all over! O glorious white marbled lady! I shall never get over you! I haven't been the same man since I met you!" All this from the man who he sees himself sitting on Shakespeare's shoulders, untouchable even by God, and I am not fit to clean his boots! *(after a moment)* Everyone wants to know whether we 'tucked up' together! Well, what does it matter now?

Perhaps it would have been better if I had been kinder to him, as Ellen Terry was. "But a gentle heart and tongue that is, do not make the best company in the world…" I forget the rest. He threatens prison if I do publish, and then what would happen to poor Moonbeam? Our roles reversed: Moonbeam visiting me in human quarantine!

Yet, love runs through every line he writes, even the harshest. *(beat)* But I could do with the pennies. I've to sell my house in England once again, and tell my daughter, sister and brother, that I can no longer support them. *(then quietly)* And Beo. Well, Beo had debts I've still to pay. Oh, what to do, what to do!

(moving about restlessly) Possibly, on occasion, I have been a horrible leading lady, and word might have reached him of this fact. Alexander? Spreading falsehood? I wouldn't put it past him. But to see Joey one last time… the man who was once my Shaw, my Joey, that would make that meal of macaroni a banquet! *(she composes herself)* He did, finally, after years of begging, offer me a script! A reward, at last, for all those years of inspiration. Pushing fifty I was at least five years too old to play her, but I knew my abilities, as did he, and realized there was meat on them bones. Not to start with, but by the last curtain, Eliza has become truly liberated. An ideal woman. I knew, as I did with Paula Tanqueray, that nobody else could or should play her.

At the first reading of *Pygmalion*, I told Mr. Herbert Beerbohm Tree, who was to be my producer and the first of my many Higginses, that I was the only actress in the West End who could pull this part off and that I wanted £130 a week with two and a half percent of the receipts! He was rather taken aback but agreed to my Shylock terms and off we went, with Joey in the director's chair. *(rises. Pulls some notes from one of the scripts on the trunk)* And I have to say I earned every penny!

Mr. Tree was cut from the same cloth as Alexander, and I could see he would side with Joey at any opportunity. School room tactics! Let's bully the little woman.

And what of my Joey in all this? What of working with Mr. Shaw? He plays games. Games with emotions as well as intellect. In both cases I am not an equal adversary. My stage notes from Shaw, April 1914. *(she reads:)*

1. When Higgins says "Oh, by the way Eliza", you must bridle your fatal propensity to run like your dog Georgina to anyone who calls you.

2. You must pay particular attention to "Thenk you koindly, laidy", "Never yeow moind","Te-oo baynches o' violets", and, most importantly, "Lawza Deulittle"!

3. Your "Don't e smell orrid" is bad.

4. There are some dreadfully middle-aged moments: you are forty years too old for this part, but there's nothing we can do about it!

I could go on, but I won't. Somebody should have shut him up as a child! Or better still, smothered him! Or better still than that: wished Marie Stopes as his mother! *(a beat)* Perhaps we should not have met; he seems happier fiddling with his women on paper.

Over the segment we hear the shock and applause of the first night audience.

It was after playing Eliza Doolittle that I was referred to as the reason society has lost its standards! As the first night drew near, there was talk that the Lord Chamberlain might storm the theatre, stop the performance! The house was sold out, had been for weeks! Word circulating London that Mrs. Patrick Campbell was going to make theatrical history. But I stuck to my guns – to be a great actress you must have a little of the gutter about you – and the line remained. Eliza is asked by Freddy – opening the door for her – *"Are you walking across the Park, Miss Doolittle?* "Walk!" Eliza replies. *"Not bloody likely! I am going in a taxi!"* Exit Eliza. *Sensation!*

There was an intake of breath, like a hiss – and I thought 'Oh Lord!' This time Stella, you really have gone too far – and then...the laughter, deafening, simply deafening, to be followed by applause! It went on forever it seemed! I was right to resist the Lord Chamberlain's wish to alter '*bloody*' to '*ruddy*' and right to fend off Beerbohm-Tree's desire to sugar the blow! The man is a buffoon! He holds two lumps of sugar inside each of his cheeks, with which he tries to sweeten one's performance! *(she is thrilled by the memory of it all)* Oh, for one more moment such as that though! The bravery to resist such sentimentality. The fearlessness to present the explosive truth.

(as she speaks, sounds of battle, lights dim) And then another war happened – how men love to play soldiers. How many wars can one live through? I had to send my men to it: Beo, and my new husband George Cornwallis-West, recently acquired. That hateful, bloody war... Joey was up in arms about it. All they want to do is "Kill! Kill! Kill!" he screamed in rehearsals! I didn't want to think about it, couldn't bear to... *(she begins to break down)* ...couldn't bear ...couldn't bear that it took another from me... my beautiful Beo, my darling baby, my beautiful, beautiful boy... I will *not* believe it... To this day I will not believe he is gone. And what good did it do? What good was it for? In Austria, women are scrubbing the streets!

The noise intensifies until it reaches a pitch. She clasps her hands to her ears. Long pause. She lifts Moonbeam from his case and cradles him.

Of all the griefs a mother has to bear the greatest is the loss of her child. *(beat)* There seemed to be no light any more... *(in time she replaces Moonbeam who stirs, her anger growing vehement)* Unfortunately, my new husband George *did* survive: war always picks the wrong men to take for his own. As the years passed, how I would have traded his worthless life for Beo's, again and again. I would trade anyone's, anyone's – save my Moonbeam's – for my beautiful boy to return! I christened husband George my 'Golden Pheasant', and how I wish him hanging with the pheasants in a cellar!

Fool that I am, three parts fool, I was easily deceived, taken in by this handsome bird. He was so attentive, charming, young, and so willing to look after everything for me, all those little business trivialities I find so tiresome... like my finances! Things of course changed, I should have seen they would. He realized he had married an old woman and I soon discovered I had an adventurer for a husband. He was like a lot of men: talked big, acted small and moved sideways. My mother once told me "A woman's eyes are not open when she is loved until she is cheated". I suppose men are the reason we women have a sense of humour? Most people have a George in their lives. Beware of him! *(cold, she puts on her cloak)* Ah, what does it matter now, it's all gone. I just long for one last hurrah, instead of being merely this monument in black velvet.

Trains leaving and departing the station again. She remains watching them for a moment. Once more she ventures to the edge of the platform.

(music as:) Stations: they are the end of the world. They make me think of suicide: Tolstoy's influence I suppose?

(pause. Music continues **STELLA** *looks over the edge of the platform. Slowly:)* Tolstoy, or Ibsen. After all Hedda takes her life as well. Strange to think two of my greatest successes, Hedda and Paula, make their own end... at least Eliza got to take her cab! *(she chuckles, moving away)*

By the time I was sixty, I'd squeezed all I could out of playing Eliza Doolittle. Joey said my Eliza had a face like a leg of mutton and her voice was all gin and misery. The cad! And not even sending a few quid when I need it most.

I had to implement new economies: Sold my car, sacked my maid and had my legendary tresses cut and shingled: it made the headlines! Though I wondered afterwards why I bothered: London wanted flappers and I couldn't flap! One young critic told me recently to retire to my cottage with my scrapbooks. "Bad though the play was," he wrote, "Mrs. Patrick Campbell's acting was worse. Neither bewitchment nor singularity make a great actress!" That was the cruelest thing anybody has ever said to me. I used to think that the great battle of life was fought in youth – all that early struggle: no money, Pat away, those nights spent making my costumes in unkempt boarding houses – but I was wrong; it is when we are old and our work not wanted, old and shabby, tired and chucked out, that the battle rages like a fire.

Pause. Music. **STELLA** *is still. An announcement is made. She takes little notice – caught up in her thoughts, she pets Moonbeam, moves up and down, then, somewhat brighter, she raises her skirts a little.*

(chuckling:) Gielgud said to me recently that he thought I have nice ankles – that was a boon. Though I wouldn't have thought he would be interested. We were rehearsing Ibsen's *Ghosts*.

I knew the young cast thought I was past it, but I bided my time, behaved well, was prompt at rehearsal and bothered to know my lines – my secretary had copied them out in large letters in an exercise book for me, my eyes are getting terrible – and there I sat on the stage, to them a relic of a bygone era. *(she sits on the bench. The lights have dimmed to a pool about her)* I was very interested to see how these babes would cope (I being an interpreter and champion of Ibsen), and I held my tongue until the director, a youth, decided to cut a certain line of Geilgud's. I told the young fellow: "No! It is the essence of Oswald's character!" I told Johnny to keep still, gaze at me and deliver the line in a channel-steamer voice, as if he were going to be sick. I then reply:

"It's all been a horrible fancy, nothing but imagination. All this excitement has been too much for you. But now you shall rest. Rest here at home, my darling son. You shall have everything you want just as you did when you were a little boy. There now. It's all over. You see how quickly it's passed".

(a beat. The lights come up softly) The line stayed in; you can't argue with genius. People forget it was I who placed Mr. Ibsen's name on the tongues of the London theatre going public. Before I picked him up he was shunned, scorned…seen as sordid. It was I who recognized an artist, whose work I could interpret. Not that anyone will remember the fact – if I were a man, oh yes, but a poor old brute in petticoats? Never! Being in this profession takes courage, understanding it takes intelligence, succeeding in it takes a pair of trousers!

I know every line, comma and full stop of a play. The step, the gesture, the word. One must get it all mechanically before one can even try and bring the emotion through. Those babes, like that director, will need that when they are working for £3 a week in trash!

I'd get back to England and stay there if it wasn't for those filthy quarantine officials! *(she collects Moonbeam up and kisses him)* They threw Moonbeam in a basket the last time and marked him 'rabies!' I stayed with my baby all night, listened to the suffering of all the others. No play, no treats, nobody to call their names. Watched as the tears in their eyes congealed to jelly and knew I had to put my little husband before career and country. And the French adore dogs – they don't eat them like they do their horses. And at least here there are still a few hotel managers who will give me a room on the strength of my name and be discreet about my bills...

And what roles are on offer to me in England, anyway? Henry Arthur Jones – a common little playwright, not an artist at all – wrote a part for me recently and then withdrew it. He read the script to me, Lord only knows why, for his accent is decidedly everyman, very south of the river; he then asked my opinion: "Too long, Mr. Jones," was my reply, "even without the aitches!"

An announcement proclaiming the train to Pau will be ready to leave in ten minutes. STELLA *is overjoyed and relieved. Music.*

Hurrah! Red letter day! Oh my! At last! At last! Oh! Oh! We are on our way, my darling, we are on our way!

She kisses Moonbeam passionately before placing him on the platform and packing up hurriedly and untidily. As she does so:

And almost morning. Waiting is one of the few great talents I have still to acquire! Hurry, Stella, hurry, we must be prepared: the step, the gesture, the word! Pau, Pau: our new home! *(she stops a moment)* And I have met the English clergyman in Pau. He was in Paris recently dealing with refugees; he says there is room enough for me in the cemetery, and is enquiring as to the whereabouts of dog lovers in the area. For one who has created such chaos in life, I have death rather in order!

She continues to stuff things away. Sounds of a train approaching. Above the din:

Alas, he had no idea who I was, but I was pleased to see he was good looking – I should hate to be buried by anyone who was ugly! *(she has finished)* Done! Perhaps it is just as well I am merely Mrs. Cornwallis-West to him – I have never divorced the Pheasant, much to his annoyance – for who is there left who remembers Mrs. Patrick Campbell? So many have passed: Pinero, Sara, Ellen, Ibsen, Tree, even that bore Alexander. Joey, only Joey remains. Yet, I am destined to be a mere footnote on his name. He says I should write a book and call it 'Though I was a wonderful Actress, no one would engage me twice'. Well I'm done with him: many, many people have engaged me twice! Perhaps I will sell those letters! Sell and be damned!

See how he likes that. That would make him blush, even beneath that filthy beard!

The noise of the train intensifies. She dons her hat. Looks down at Moonbeam and scoops him up under her arm.

But we still rally, don't we Moonbeam? We can still be proud of this chance medley of a life. *(picks up her cane and begins to search for a porter)* And I hear there is an English Theatre in Pau: an engagement perhaps? They will insist on my playing, I'm sure. With just enough to buy sandwiches for you and me, eh Moonbeam? A season of Hedda? Or Eliza, perhaps? A provincial audience would accept the age difference. Oh, for just one more red letter day! Porter! Porter! …Thank heavens! He's managed to winkle himself away from that lonely looking woman in the waiting room. *(to a porter, pointing to her luggage with her cane)* These and all these. And then, Monsieur, there are – *(realizing that Moonbeam has urinated on the platform while she was packing, and the porter and other passengers have noticed, she hears them and becomes indignant)* Oh Moonbeam, is that tiddles? Oh baby. *(she stifles a laugh, picking him up)* Naughty! *(grandly to the crowd)* Well, what are you all looking at? I did it! *(she composes herself)* Now, don't forget the cases! Come along, Moonbeam, let us go in search of new adventures. We are not all cold ashes at the bottom of the grate, yet. There is still a little of the roaring fire left!

MRS. PATRICK CAMPBELL *hugs Moonbeam tightly, turns and begins to exit. As she does so the noise of the station and the train, preparing to leave, increases and smoke and steam obliterate them from view. Lights fade to black. Music fades in. Slow curtain.*

The End

Property List

Act 1

Bench (p1)

In the distance: Porters' trolleys and luggage and a waiting room just visible (p1)

Vast iron framework of station (p1)

A large standing travelling trunk (p1)

Three hat boxes – one of which is black and vast (p1)

A typewriter (p1)

Smaller trunk (p1)

Small suitcase (p1)

Other pieces of luggage are nearby (p1)

Coverlet (p8)

She opens the trunk. It is crammed with clothes, letters, books and memorabilia (p8)

Hand mirror (p8)

Folded napkin containing some past-their-best grapes (p9)

Large sheet of paper (p9)

Some letters (p10)

She removes the small drawer and places it on her lap (p11)

Cooked chicken (p16)

Act 2

A copy of Hedda Gabler lies open on top of a number of scripts on the main trunk (p20)

Cushioned suitcase (p20)

A pistol (p20)

Small bustle of passengers (p22)

Envelope with cooked chicken inside (p23)

Reading a letter plucked randomly (p23)

Pulls some notes from one of the scripts on the trunk (p24)

Lighting

Act 1

Lights up very slowly (p1)

On a dim stage a bench is gradually lit (p1)

As she speaks the lighting changes to something more intimate and theatrical (p2)

The lights revert to the station lighting as before (p5)

The lights change, moving from box to box etc. (p6)

She rises and the lights revert to the general light of the platform (p6)

As she speaks the lighting creates the effect of a bright follow spot (p7)

The follow spot and music dim (p7)

The lights change (p8)

Face picks up the light again (p8)

The lights intensify (p10)

The lights dim (p11)

The lights brighten (p13)

The lights dim (p14)

The lights flicker, as in a Victorian melodrama (p15)

The lights close in (p16)

The lights close in (17)

Lights fade (p19)

Act 2

Lights up (p20)

Lights change (p21)

Lights dim (p26)

The lights have dimmed to a pool around her (p28)

The lights come up softly (p28)

Lights fade to black (p30)

Effects

Act 1

Music (p1)

Sounds of trains, guards, whistles etc. (p1)

An announcement is made that the train from Toulouse to Pau will be delayed in arriving and to await further announcements (p1)

Sounds of chatter, popping flashbulbs (p3)

A projector runs (p5)

Fade in party music (p5)

The follow spot and music dim (p5)

Projector runs (p8)

Distant sound of trains (p10)

Music (p10)

Train announcements and sounds of trains arriving and leaving the station becomes louder (p10)

Smoke, steam etc. (p10)

Music (p12)

In time, street sounds fade in and out (p13)

The faint sound of an audience, which grows and reacts to the incident on stage and then becomes applause (p14)

Train announcements (p15)

Music (p15)

Pause as further announcements are made (p18)

Music (p18)

Music (p19)

Act 2

Music (p20)

We hear the pop of flashbulbs and the blur of a crowd of reporters and fans (p21)

An announcement (p22)

Music (p22)

We hear shock and applause from the first night audience (p25)

As she speaks, the sounds of battle (p26)

The noise intensifies until it reaches pitch (p26)

Trains leaving and departing the station again (p27)

Music (p27)

Music continues (p27)

Music (p27)

An announcement is made (p27)

An announcement proclaiming the train to Pau will be ready to leave in ten minutes (p29)

Music (p29)

Sound of a train approaching (p29)

The noise of the train intensifies (p29)

Moonbeam has urinated on the platform (p30)

The noise of the station and the train, preparing to leave, increases and smoke and steam obliterate them from view (p30)

Music fades in (p30)

Slow curtain (p30)

Costumes

Act 1

She wears a dark cloak with a fur collar, (upon which is pinned a bunch of wilting violets), a hat, and she carries an aging, monstrous looking Pekinese Dog – Moonbeam – under one arm; her hands are encased in tattered gloves. She uses a cane (more for effect than necessity) (p1)

Act 2

Stella, without her cloak (tossed aside) has added a vibrant, worn winter shawl to her costume (p20)